A Beginner's Guide to raising Turkeys

Raising Turkeys in Your Backyard for Pleasure and Profit

Country Life Books

Dueep Jyot Singh

Mendon Cottage Books

JD-Biz Publishing

Disclaimer

The information is this book is provided for informational purposes only. It is not intended to be used and medical advice or a substitute for proper medical treatment by a qualified health care provider. The information is believed to be accurate as presented based on research by the author.

The contents have not been evaluated by the U.S. Food and Drug Administration or any other Government or Health Organization and the contents in this book are not to be used to treat cure or prevent disease.

The author or publisher is not responsible for the use or safety of any diet, procedure or treatment mentioned in this book. The author or publisher is not responsible for errors or omissions that may exist.

Warning

The Book is for informational purposes only and before taking on any diet, treatment or medical procedure, it is recommended to consult with your primary health care provider.

Check out some of the other Healthy Gardening Series books at Amazon.com

Gardening Series on Amazon

Check out some of the other Health Learning Series books at Amazon.com

Health Learning Series on Amazon

Table of Contents

Introduction

Did you know that turkeys are native to the New World- i.e North America, and have been around for millenniums? So, is it a wonder that when these delicious and pompous birds reached the shores of Europe in the 16th century, thanks to the traders in West Indies and Spain, they were immediately added to exotic and popular fare. And since then, a turkey dinner, especially on Thanksgiving and on Christmas was soon a part of the social fabric.

Turkeys may not be eaten as often as you eat chicken, but you can always have them for Turkey sandwiches. Turkish traders and merchants brought them to Europe by ship, and that is why the name "turkey" became synonymous with this unusually funny looking and self-important birds strutting about in your backyard.

Once upon a time there were also called the Indian fowl. I was under the impression that that was because the Native Americans were called Indians at that time. They knew the value of this bird and hunted it regularly.

That was until I found out that the "Indian" part of the name came from the European tendency of naming exotic birds, with the names of exotic lands. So the Catalans called it *Gall d'inde* and the French also called it *Poulet d'inde* meaning fowl from India.

 In Hebrew, it is called *Tarnegol Hodu* – rooster of India. And the irony is that in Turkey, it is called *Hindi* which means related to India! In reality, Indians of India did not know about this bird until the Britishers brought it to India for their turkey dinners in the late 18th and 19th century.

But these are native birds living for millenniums in the North American continent. Wild turkeys also known to the first settlers as "gobblers" soon became a part of the dining table, and the Puritans must have been really surprised at such a show of pomp and colorful splendor in a gobbler.

Wild turkeys

Turkey Varieties

The original birds were black and soon breeders started domesticating them with crossing them with wild North American turkeys and re-crossing them with more wild species. Breeders in Rhode Island made a variety called the Narragansett, – a metallic black in color with the ends of the feathers smart with light gray verging on white.

In America the light fawn to cinnamon brown with white in the wings and tail, and the bourbon red , a dark brownish red color with wing and tail feathers almost white, were also developed. When you blended white and bronze varieties, you would get the buff colored variety.

These breeders also developed the white, and although it was called the white Holland and white Austrian, it is a mixture of colors ranging from black, bronze and gray.

The American Slate is slaty- blue in color. It comes from a blend of black and bronze with buff and white.

American bronze turkeys are normally called American mammoths in Turkey shows. These mammoths weight up to 35 pounds for Turkey cockerels, cock birds 35 – 50 pounds, pullets 14 – 22 pounds and hens 18 – 26 pounds.

You may find some really good specimens up to 40 pounds in shows! That is supposedly the standardized weight for healthy birds which come in the ultra large category. The smaller full breasted table variety weighs less and that is what you are going to get in the market.

A young Bronze Tom bird should weigh around 25 pounds. A yearling should be around 33 pounds, an adult Tom bird 36 pounds, a young hen 16 pounds, a yearling hen – 18 pounds and an adult hen- 20 pounds. We normally do not get such fine birds in the market, because they are being mass produced, and nobody is bothering much about taking care about fattening them to their limits.

But when you try your hand at turkey farming, remember I have told you the weights to which they can grow. So you can try aiming at that particular weight goal.

You may also want to try breeding small family turkeys. They weigh less – males weigh 14 – 18 pounds, females weigh nine – 11 pounds. The average weight of a turkey should be anywhere between 10 pounds to 30 pounds. So, depending on the size of your turkey dinner, look at the variety you want to raise.

Ultra large Thanksgiving and Christmas birds are going to be mammoth bronzes. But as microwaves and ovens become smaller, those turkey farmers catering for smaller Christmas turkeys have devoted serious attention to black, white, and blue varieties.

In America, it is customary to eat turkey throughout the year, – and not only on special occasions and festive days – especially in sliced sandwich and snacks. So if you are thinking of raising turkeys in your backyard as a hobby, think about a healthy source of homegrown meat, for your family. You may also find yourself building a turkey ranch!

How to Choose the Best Turkeys for Breeding

Quality standards should be adhered to strictly, when you are choosing breeding birds to keep the flock up to a high average standard of merit. This is, of course, if you are raising turkeys for business or show purposes. Even if you are breeding them for table purposes, you need to look for turkeys which are compact, well-balanced and healthy looking individuals.

Take note of the legs and feet, aiming at strongly built and well-rounded shanks, straight and wide apart. The toes should be straight, strong, and well apart. Avoid those birds with an awkward gait, clumsy action, heavy feet, crooked toes, twisted feet, curved outer toes back toes off the ground or turned towards the front.

A healthy bird is going to stand narrow and in- kneed with flat sides, narrowness across the shoulders and with a shallow high pointed breast bone. The body shape should be long, deep, and well rounded. The back should be broad and flat between the shoulders and with well-rounded sides.

A turkey is primarily a table bird so you need to pay strict attention to table merits. The actual breastbone should be long and straight, without any curve or crooked defect and without the high and undesirable knob at the point. The fleshing in the breast should be deep, broad and well rounded.

An ideal bird is also going to have medium length of leg, with well-rounded and full-fleshed thighs, carrying ample fleshing of fine quality meat and skin, the latter also of attractive color and the bones generally not too heavy.

The best table birds are those birds which are rapid growers, featherers and fleshers.

Rapid growth rate is essential when you are building up a healthy flock of turkeys for the cable. All of these are going to have some common factors – early maturity, economic feeding for the meat poundage gain, maximum egg yields, good hatchability and rearability.

Examine, and weigh your chickens for feathering and fleshing at 12, 16, 20 and 24 weeks for stags and 12, 16 and 20 weeks for female pullets. This is because the females are going to mature a month earlier than the males and you can set aside the best for stock breeding birds.

This URL can give you more information about the common turkey breeds available in America.

http://www.the-perfect-turkey.com/turkey-breeds.html

A good healthy young turkey chick is going to be bright eyed healthy specimen, hatched with a solid body front, deep strong face and beak, healthy legs and balanced proportions.

Egg Production

The natural laying season of turkeys start about March, the turkey laying two batches of eggs. Each of these batches are going to contain 25 eggs. She is going to go broody in between.

If she is isolated when she is broody, she is going to restart laying. The old custom is to let ordinary hens sit and hatch the first clutch of eggs and the turkey on the second lot.

You may want to try that out if you want to raise turkey chicks.

Broody hens are good for incubating turkey chicks

Cockerels mated with pullets are going to give table offspring. Mate them early in January or late in December and treat the stock season as from February to May, continuing into June for the Christmas trade. Birds which are hatched later are going to have smaller carcasses. This late hatching is going to suit all those who put turkey eggs through their incubators when they have finished the season for ordinary poultry chicks.

In the smaller plump table turkey bird types, some early hatched pullets will start laying in autumn. Sometimes laying may not start until the end of February for larger pullets and in March for hens.

So how many eggs should you expect from Turkeys? Pullets are going to start laying earlier than adult hens. Smaller type pullets lay over hundred eggs in a season, starting from March.

There are some farmers, who try to provide their birds with a 15 hour day with lighting at night. 5 Hundred watt bulbs are placed in the birds pens, and this increases and brings forward the egg production especially when the

birds are put in roomy enclosure with   protective banks of baled straw
around the pens and deep straw on the ground.

Incubation of Turkey Eggs

Turkey eggs normally take approximately 28 days to incubate and the
number that can be put into a 150 chicken incubator is 120 turkey eggs,
depending on their size.

The fertility and hatchability percent is going to depend on the condition of
the parent birds, their individual selection and a degree and also the season.

If you have hundred breeding birds, you are going to get 80 to 90 chickens from each small incubating machine from the beginning of spring to the end of May on an exposed farm.

Depending on the breed, individual hatchlings can vary between 70 – 90%, which indicate the importance of good breeding and selection so that you get birds which are going to lay healthy eggs from which the hatchability rate is high.

The temperature of your incubator should be 10 3°F with the thermometer just above the top of the eggs.

There are so many incubators available in the market today, which are running carefully at 10 4°F, which also gives a good hatchability rate.

If you have put the eggs in the incubator, remember to turn them regularly after sprinkling them lightly with lukewarm water. This is necessary when you are using a hot-air incubator. This turning is done twice daily from the start to the cracking of the shell of the first egg.

In cold weather, turning is quick, and the floor of the incubator shed is not watered. But in warm weather, the floor is sprinkled with water. When the eggs started to crack, sprinkle more warm water. The empty shells should be removed weekly during hatching.

Near the hatch, in warm weather number you door of the incubator is left open for one hour cool down and the windows and doors of the sheds are also opened. In very hot weather, the lamp should be put out for periods to ensure a steady temperature and prevent it from going too high, especially during the last few days.

Turkey eggs need more moisture than chicken eggs and duck eggs, and a steady temperature is essential. You may want to go in for 103.5° throughout.

For quick and successful hatch offs, always set eggs which are not over three days old. After this, the hatching result is going to deteriorate, especially when you have transported the eggs from one place to another.

Store the eggs in a cool, damp-ish place for a couple of days, but take them into the incubator room the day before they are to be set.

Do not place cold eggs into the empty incubator as too high a temperature otherwise you are going to have eggs with broken yolks. That is going to reduce the hatchability percentage

If they are to be stored more than three or four days, place the eggs on their sides in drawers, protected from the weather, and turn them morning and evening.

When the chickens are hatched and dry, they can be allowed down into the nursery under the egg tray, which is going to be withdrawn at the conclusion of the hatch.

You can also take them out when dry in batches instead of putting them in the nursery, and place them in another safer place.

Test the eggs for fertility on the 10th day of incubation by removing all the clear eggs and marking the doubtful eggs which are going to be removed along with the addled eggs on the second test, taking place on the 15th day.

How to Test Turkey Eggs

You can either lift up the eggs, and hold them against a source of light, or if your eggs are placed on a wire mesh, you can pass a torch underneath them. If the eggs are healthy, you are going to see a shadow which means that the chicken is growing inside the egg. If the eggs are clear, that means they are no chickens and the eggs need to be taken out from the clutch.

Natural Incubation.

1 day old turkey poult.

A turkey hen is a very reliable sitter and mother, covering up to 16 or so eggs and covering a considerable number of chickens.

Let the turkey select its own nesting place and put up a netting surround to keep the male turkey away as it is often spiteful to chicks.

Provide water, dried dust bath, and grain trough, feeding just once daily. Make sure the turkey is undisturbed.

Ordinary broody hens are used for sitting and rearing on a clutch of 8 to 10 eggs, according to the season, the size of the eggs and the size of the hen.

A healthy and well fleshed hen, which is also well feathered is going to last 28 days, and all the eggs must be covered when it is sitting.

Broody hens are going to bring of more chicks than the incubator, but they must be dusted thoroughly with insect powder before being set. That is because young turkey chicks are prone to lice and become unprofitable, when attacked by such pests.

Prepare a sitting box with a small mesh, wire netted bottom as a precaution against rats and make the nest of earth with straw around and in the corners and small cut straw in the middle.

Hand turn the eggs in the morning and the evening and let the hen off for a meal, each morning, sprinkling the eggs with warm water daily, before her return, and more so when the first egg is chipped. This is when the outings are going to stop. The nesting materials and the corners of the box also have to be watered.

Provide a dust bath, drinking water, food trough and grit.

You can use the rearing Coop as a sitting box, and have a wire topped run attached with the sides and the ends boarded.

Housing Your Birds

Never house your birds in closed and stuffy quarters. This is going to cause swollen faces or colds in your turkeys, yes, even turkeys can suffer from watery nostrils in cold weather.

You may also try the traditional method of erecting a 6 inches thick ash pole in each enclosure placed on firm end supports to take 10 hens and a stag. These birds can then sleep outdoors.

In each run, to provide nests, posts are erected and encircled with wire netting, which is going to be divided into compartments also by netting, with sacking used to cover the tops, ends and partitions while each compartment has a sacking flap for the first entrance.

You may also try selecting a tree in your garden, and make a surround of fencing. The top is going to be surmounted by a 4 x 3" watch with slightly rounded edges and a letter of poles placed against the surround for the turkeys to go up to roost.

This can be done in places where you do not have to bother about predators like Foxes and outdoor roosting is practical. Roosting can also be done in suitable tree branches so long as the ladder is placed against the tree trunk in a slanting position. Train your birds to open air roosting in the growing stages.

Span Roof

You can also make a span roof on stout supports with the sides and the ends open. You are going to place perches under it from the front to the back. A popular structure span roof is going to be with the sides and ends boarded up for 2 feet with a 2 inch mesh wire netting above it all around and the entire front being in the form of 2 white doors so that your turkeys can be driven into the roost readily.

Try making a slatted floor in sections, which is going to be fitted one foot off the boarded floor. This facilitates cleaning, especially when the perches are removable.

Lean to Roosts

Traditional lean to roosts are normally made with corrugated iron over the roof, back and ends, with two wire netting doors to open outwards, occupying the entire front .

You can also fit three or four rows of perches about 2'6" up, with a row or two of lower perches for birds who cannot fly up the higher roosting perches.

Span roof shelters often have 18 inch sides with wire netting, the roof coming almost down to the ground with both ends wire netted, one of which opens outwards. The perches are installed in it.

It has a wooden floor, and you can also fit it with skids. That is, if you want to move the turkey roost to fresh sites in your backyard.

Wire netted runs or enclosures are 5 to 6 feet high, with just one single wire along the top. Allow adult turkeys anywhere between 40 to 50 yd.^{2} of grass run or enclosure, and straw bales are going to make excellent shelters and windbreaks.

In runs, where there are no bushes and natural nesting places, particularly hedgerows, turkeys like to make their own secluded nests and straw should be placed in such likely places as laying time approaches, if one wants a new brood of turkeys.

Without natural surroundings, one needs to provide a nesting compartment for each hen.

Some Tips

Do not force the pullets and hens into off-season egg production. Bring them on gradually to lay eggs with healthy shells. Do not fatten the adult hens and cocks, and in the off-season do not feed the adult birds too generously, particularly the males.

Harden the birds in the resting season. The over fat hens are going to lay smaller eggs as well as shell less eggs.

Give the breeding birds plenty of green leafy vegetables like cabbage, kale, grated raw carrots and finely chopped onion tops and chives.

On a gravel soil, they are going to get enough flint and grit, but this can also be heaped in each run, where it is thought necessary, together with a heap or box of limestone grit or shelling material, especially as laying time approaches and also clean water to drink at all times.

A healthy organic breeder's mash is made up of 10 pounds bran, 35 pounds of middlings-the material which is left over when we process wheat in a mill-, grass meal – 5 pounds, ground oats – 15 pounds, corn meal – 20 pounds, dried yeast 3 pounds, mineral mixture – 2 pounds and fish meal – 10 pounds.

Ranging Baby Turkeys

Turkey chicks are best ranged over fresh clean grass or a leafy growth of red clover. The brooding unit measures 6'3" long by 4'3" width, 3 feet high in front and 2 feet at the back, and it can be put on wheels. It has a sliding lid, a slide along glass window over a netted aperture in the front and a number of adjustable slides for ventilation.

You can either have boarded floors or slatted floors.

Attached to this is a 10 feet by 4 feet sectional run, covered at the top, sides and end with an inch mesh wire netting, and with a service door on top.

An exit is present in the end of the house, which leads to the detachable fold run. You can move the entire unit daily to fresh grass, depending on the availability of this grass. A number of units can be arranged in a row.

In the end of the rearing unit, you can place a 100 chicks size hover, the boarded floor of which is littered down.

A metal surrounded front of the hover is going to form a cozy spot at first for food and water. This is also going to train the chicks to go under the hover for warmth, as required, instead of hunting in corners and getting chilled.

You can place 100 healthy chicks, in it in the initial stages, and reduce the number to 50 later on, and to 30 at 8 to 10 weeks of age. This is when perches are introduced and the hover taken out after weaning.

This dry, warm and airy housing is essential with the young turkey chicks protected against cold, damp litter and showers. Find chopped straw is a good litter, and the base can be fine, dry River sand and Peat Moss.

They are going to need plenty of heat under the hover at the start, slightly over 90°F midway between the heater and the outside walls of the hover. If they huddle around the heater, they are going to get cold.

You can use curtains around the sides of the hover at the start and gradually remove them singly, from the back, at first to allow more air.

Keep the chicks near to the heat for the first seven days or so and then keep reducing by 5° weekly, according to the weather, weaning them away gradually at 6 to 8 weeks at which age they are less affected by weather changes.

Continuing the folding system as a carry-on, the span roof house is 7 feet long by 6 feet wide, 6 feet high at the Ridge and 3 feet high at the eaves. Apart from lower boarding all around, the parts about are wire netted, at the ends and sides with adjustable slide up shutters to the sides and ends.

Five 4" x 3" perches are installed and 8" x 2.5" iron wheels are fitted on 3" x 2" axles. To this is attached to wire netting run, 17, eight long by 6 feet wide and 3 feet high, which is built on a strongly braced frame of 2" x 1.5" and is covered by 1 inch netting on the top sides and at the end with the service door in the top.

The base is going to be fitted with 4.5" x 2" skid type runners. The floor of the house is boarded. The four runs are detachable, so that the entire unit can be moved to fresh grass daily. Such a unit takes 30 turkeys to maturity and on a 10 acre field, you can have up to 1000 turkeys reared to maturity on this fold system and on clover.

Containers for Food

Do not permit any overcrowding at the containers, because that is going to cause uneven growth among these chickens. Increase the eating space systematically has the chickens get larger, bringing in many standardized utensils.

Square and wooden trays are excellent, for baby chicks. You can clean them up easily and replace them.

A 2 feet long wooden box, about 2 inches high In front, and 4 inches at the back, a depth of 8 inches from front to back and fitted with a lid is going to hold mash and starter pellets.

A one and a half inches wide slat goes along the bottom of the lid as a lid to prevent any wastage of mood and another slat 1 inch deep is fixed along the top of the lid, leaving the intervening aperture for feeding, although a hinged part can also permit control by closing the aperture.

Double-sided mash troughs are practical, when the chickens grow up. Fit them with "lips" to prevent waste. Keep food off the litter for young turkeys or they may start eating the material laid out on the ground.

The water fountain should not be deep enough for young chicks to get drowned and should later be placed on a wire topped frame to prevent damp litter, with a baking tin beneath it to catch any dripping water. Circular wire grids can also prevent the chicks from getting into the containers.

When the turkeys started growing up a bit, green food is suspended from the top of the wire netted for them to peck and thus they can keep busy throughout the day.

You can also place it in a suspended string bag or in a rack outside the wire netting by just adding another piece of netting, arranged outside like a bag. This is an excellent arrangement, especially if you are raising turkeys in veranda or raised balcony.

In such a case, outside feeding and watering arrangements are adopted, with the birds putting their heads through the space between slats or wooden spars to reach the food and water.

Metal troughs can also be pivoted to turn outside for filling and back again into the pen. Thus you can save a lot of labor. It has been claimed that 3000 turkeys can be read on a farm of 1 acre in wire floored pens.

Turkey chicks should be raised on clean and fresh land each year, and never be allowed to go on the ground which has been used by adult birds. You can also allow them to follow land which has been plowed up to get their share of insect meal.

Feeding Your Turkeys

Three feeds are customary, with some people giving their birds breeder pellets available in the market morning and afternoon, and green for the last meal and others give them a wet mash in the morning, breeder pellets in the afternoon, and grain green in the evening.

A daily minimum requirement of four to 6 ounces of mash or pellets and 2 – 3 ounces of grains per adult on range is often recommended, but turkeys are quite capable of asking more if they are underfed.

Give all these birds food in troughs, each about 6 feet long, 5 ½ deep and 10 to 12 inches wide, with a hole bored in each end of the troughs to let out rainwater and with stout end supports.

The best grain mixture is of wheat grain and oats, but perhaps a little barley added.

Fattening Your Turkey Chicks

Here comes the holiday season, and there is not any reason why Turkey chicks should not be fattened for a delicious Thanksgiving or Christmas dinner. The choice of the feeding system is going to depend on the food stuffs available to you.

This is going to include wet mash and grain, dry mash and grain, wet and dry mash and grain, pellets, the lead sand grain, dry mash, pellets and grain, and wet match collects and grain.

At first the turkey chicks are shy feeders and you can place a number of ordinary ordinary chicks with each batch to teach them how to eat.

Dip the beaks of some of the turkey chicks into the drinking water, a number of times daily for the first few days.

Sprinkle a little pinhead oatmeal on their backs before the first feed and at times during the first few days. This is an old trick. They are going to peck at this and recognize it as food when it is placed on top of their mash.

Turkey chicks require ample feeding space at all ages. When they are out on shot and succulent grass, they are going to peck at their mash, wander into the pen to peck at grass and tender shoots and then retire into the brooder for a warm-up before repeating this exercise again.

Your feeding plan should make sure that they are well fleshed. Make them accustomed to being handled by you, from the very first day, so that you can check up with their weight. The materials which are going to form their bone are essential because of the heavy frames which are going to be built up continuously. High-protein mashers are favorable for several weeks from the start and nourishing food stuffs have to be given for the first 10 to 12 weeks.

Onions, chives and leaks should readily be available, grated raw carrot is very beneficial and cabbage at later stages is excellent. You can also add finely chopped dandelions, nettles, lettuce and banana leaves, onion tops, chickweed, mustard and crest, watercress, clover and tender grass as succulent green foods for growing young chicks.

A popular system for Turkey chicks on grass is to give them grated bread pieces, hard-boiled eggs, – you can use the clear eggs from the incubator here – and finely chopped chives, dandelion, and nettle leaves, or the like, for several days, three times daily with a little cracked or rolled grain, morning and evening.

Oatmeal, rolled oats, cracked and rolled wheat, and a small sized ground maize or flakes normally make an excellent grain mixture. Finally chopped green food can be rubbed into a meal mixture containing of bran – 20 pounds, middling – 30 pounds, maize meal – 25 pounds, ground oats – 20 pounds, dried yeast – 3 pounds, fish meal – 5 pounds, dried skim milk – 5 pounds and mineral salts – 2 pounds.

A small grain feed in the morning and evening is continued with three crumbly wet mashes in between, so that some is left before them for pecking when they want. Place a little bird sand on the feeding boards or in shallow mash boxes, at the start and then add chicken sized limestone, grit and crushed oyster shell for the calcium content after a month.

Four feeds daily for a month is going to be sufficient, three of mash and one of grain as the last for the day. For three months give three feeds daily, two of mash on one of grain. Cabbage and kale will then be part of the daily diet, and in plenty. Wheat, 2 to 3 measures with oats and barley, one measure of each is going to be the whole grain.

After 12 weeks, you can add steamed potatoes to the mash, about 20% for stock birds and twice the amount for table birds.

Some people also start the chicks off with a dry mash containing Chicken pellets, which is always before them, and also put finely chopped, tender, raw green food and chives and other green foods on top of the food now and then, with a sprinkling of bird sand. Dry mash and pellets with green food and small grits are continued when these chickens are raised to 10 weeks.

From 10 weeks, if you are raising them on grass range, four feeds daily are given for stock birds, of what they will eat in 30 minutes. This includes crumbly wet mash for breakfast and tea, pellets at midday and grain – oats, wheat and barley – for the evening.

From about three months, three feeds of grower pellets, wet mash and grain are given to stock birds daily. Grain is gradually increased, particularly oats.

If you are raising your chickens in a fattening pen, you are going to need a highly nourishing dry mash from the very beginning to 12 weeks with a little grain daily given twice for the first month, and after the omission of grain, to crumbly wet mashes daily with dry mash always before them.

The dry mash mixture in this case is the same as that for growers. From three months of age, the best mash is going to contain cooked potatoes, minced table scraps, etc. while green food has to be given daily. Limestone and Flint grit is included in the diet as desired.

Growers Mash

Growers mash is going to consist of 10 pounds of bran, 30 pounds of middlings, 5 pounds of grass meal, 15 pounds of cornmeal, 15 pounds of ground oats, 10 pounds of barley meal, 5 pounds of fish meal, 5 pounds of meat and bone meal, 2 pounds of mineral salts, and 3 pounds of dried yeast.

When turkeys are to be prepared for table, bring into use three wet mashes daily for several final weeks, using a meal blend of 15 pounds middling, 30 pounds of ground oats, 30 pounds of grass meal, 15 pounds of maize meal, and 10 pounds of bone meal and meat.

To this, you can add cooked potatoes and minced house scraps, boiled barley and also soaked maize flakes. Do not give any fish product during the final fattening process because this is going to cause a fishy taint in the flesh.

Soaked grain is often given to growers. Although more grain is brought in gradually from six – eight weeks, oats are not introduced until about 10 – 12 weeks, gradually and not in excess quantities.

Give green food in plenty, each turkey consuming anywhere between 4 to 6 ounces daily, when about 16 weeks old. Clover is excellent. You may want to add powdered charcoal in the mash, if the appetite seem to have gone off.

The exact quantity of food needed for each bird is determined only by trial and error, although at eight weeks, 3 ounces of mash and pellets and grain required per bird is often quoted as an approximate guide. 5 ounces from 16 weeks and heaven out from 20 weeks. Growth is very rapid, with Turkey chicks in the first month, increasing a times or more. Its body weight and over 20 times in the first eight weeks, if you give them plenty of rain especially oats.

So remember, the diet should be not too much grain, lots of protein for fleshing, meal and phosphate of lime for bone formation. Skim milk watered down is given to drink and over mashes where available. You can also add 2% cod liver oil to mash, and also other ingredients as fish meal, dried milk, dried yeast, minerals, salts, grass meal and tender green food.

Home-grown cereals can also be used when available, as turkeys like somewhat coarsely ground cereal meals. Vegetable proteins in the shape of beans and peas can also be added to grower mashes and rolled grain is highly appreciated, especially wheat.

Whole and ground buckwheat is also recommended, the meal having fattening properties. Some of the roots which are liked by turkeys include beetroot, fodder beet, parsnips and carrots.

How to Prepare a Turkey For Table

You need to use both hands to dislocate the neck of the turkey with a firm jerk upwards. Do not feed the turkey for about 12 – 15 hours to killing it. This is so that the crop can be emptied of meal.

You may want to see how a butcher prepares a Turkey, for table, before you try this yourself. Pluck the carcass immediately after killing, including all feather stubs but leave the feathers on one third of the neck, the back feathers covering the hips – to prevent bruising and the shorter feathers on the end joint of the wings.

Clear the vents of waste material and then hang the carcass for thorough cooling.

Smoked Turkey

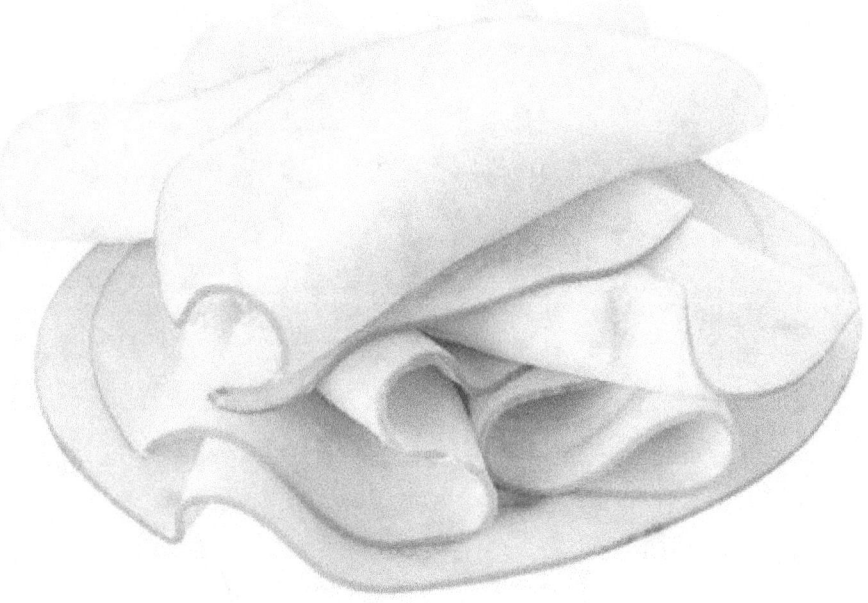

Now this is the traditional way in which whole and clean turkeys as well as their cut up parts with the skin left on can be preserved for eating. Take 75 pounds of meat in a 25 gallon barrel, place them for 10 days at a temperature of 32°F – seven days at 50/60°F – in a solution of 8 pounds of salt, 3 pounds of sugar, **3 ounces** of saltpetre – potassium nitrate/sodium nitrate, which is used extensively for preserving the shelf life of meat; both are called saltpetre – and 6 gallons of water.

The meat is then drained for 24 hours, and then wrapped up in cheesecloth and hung in a smoke room for 12 hours. 16 – 18 hours is going to give you a stronger flavor.

Hardwood sawdust is going to be used in the fire, and if the latter is controlled, the temperature at the meat level is less than 12 5°F

The uncooked and smoked turkey meat is then roasted for a time and temperature similar to that employed for fresh turkey, with frequent basting, to give you ready to eat smoked turkey.

Conclusion

This book has introduced you to the joy of raising turkeys in your own farm or backyard. As a beginner's guide, you are going to get tips and techniques about turkeys and raising them.

Turkey farming is just like the duck farming and chicken farming – only the birds are larger in size, and are going to give you more meat on the table.

Many people think Turkey farming to be a headache. But that is because they do not want to put in the time, dedication and the effort to get the satisfaction of doing a job thoroughly.

So if you know a place where you can get turkey chickens, and have some empty space around your house, start building your turkey coops. Right now, sustainable farming is the need of the hour. Learn to become self-sufficient, and once you become experienced, you are going to find this effort profitable and well worth it.

Live Long and Prosper!

Author Bio-

Dueep Jyot Singh is a Management and IT Professional who managed to gather Postgraduate qualifications in Management and English and Degrees in Science, French and Education while pursuing different enjoyable career options like being an hospital administrator, IT,SEO and HRD Database Manager/ trainer, movie , radio and TV scriptwriter, theatre artiste and public speaker, lecturer in French, Marketing and Advertising, ex-Editor of Hearts On Fire (now known as Solstice) Books Missouri USA, advice columnist and cartoonist, publisher and Aviation School trainer, ex-moderator on Medico.in, banker, student councilor ,travelogue writer … among other things!

One fine morning, she decided that she had enough of killing herself by Degrees and went back to her first love -- writing. It's more enjoyable! She already has 48 published academic and 14 fiction- in- different- genre books under her belt.

When she is not designing websites or making Graphic design illustrations for clients , she is browsing through old bookshops hunting for treasures, of which she has an enviable collection – including R.L. Stevenson, O.Henry, Dornford Yates, Maurice Walsh, De Maupassant, Victor Hugo, Sapper, C.N. Williamson, "Bartimeus" and the crown of her collection- Dickens "The Old Curiosity Shop," and so on… Just call her "Renaissance Woman") - collecting herbal remedies, acting like Universal Helping Hand/Agony Aunt, or escaping to her dear mountains for a bit of exploring, collecting herbs and plants and trekking.

Check out some of the other JD-Biz Publishing books

Gardening Series on Amazon

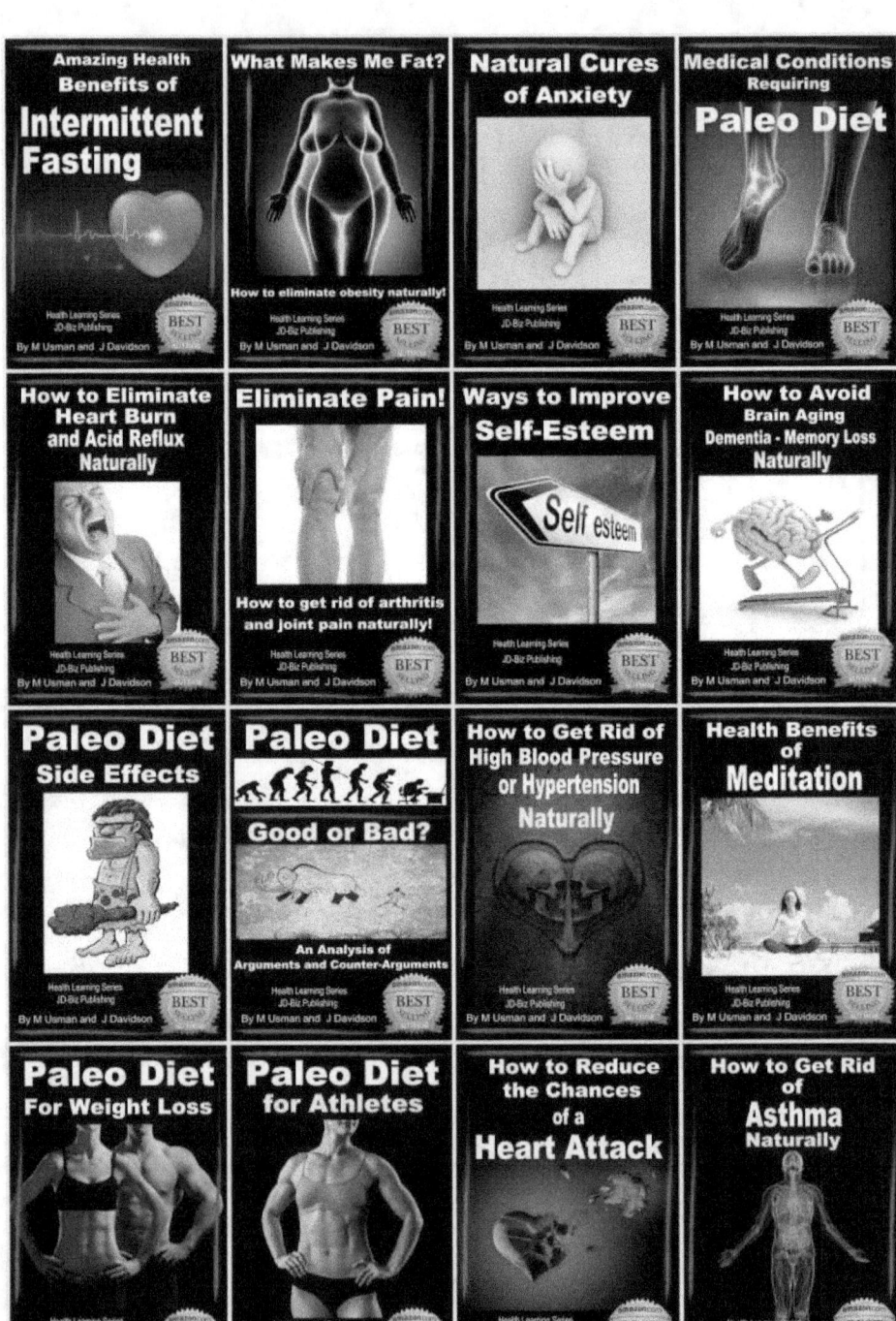

Amazing Animal Book Series

Learn To Draw Series

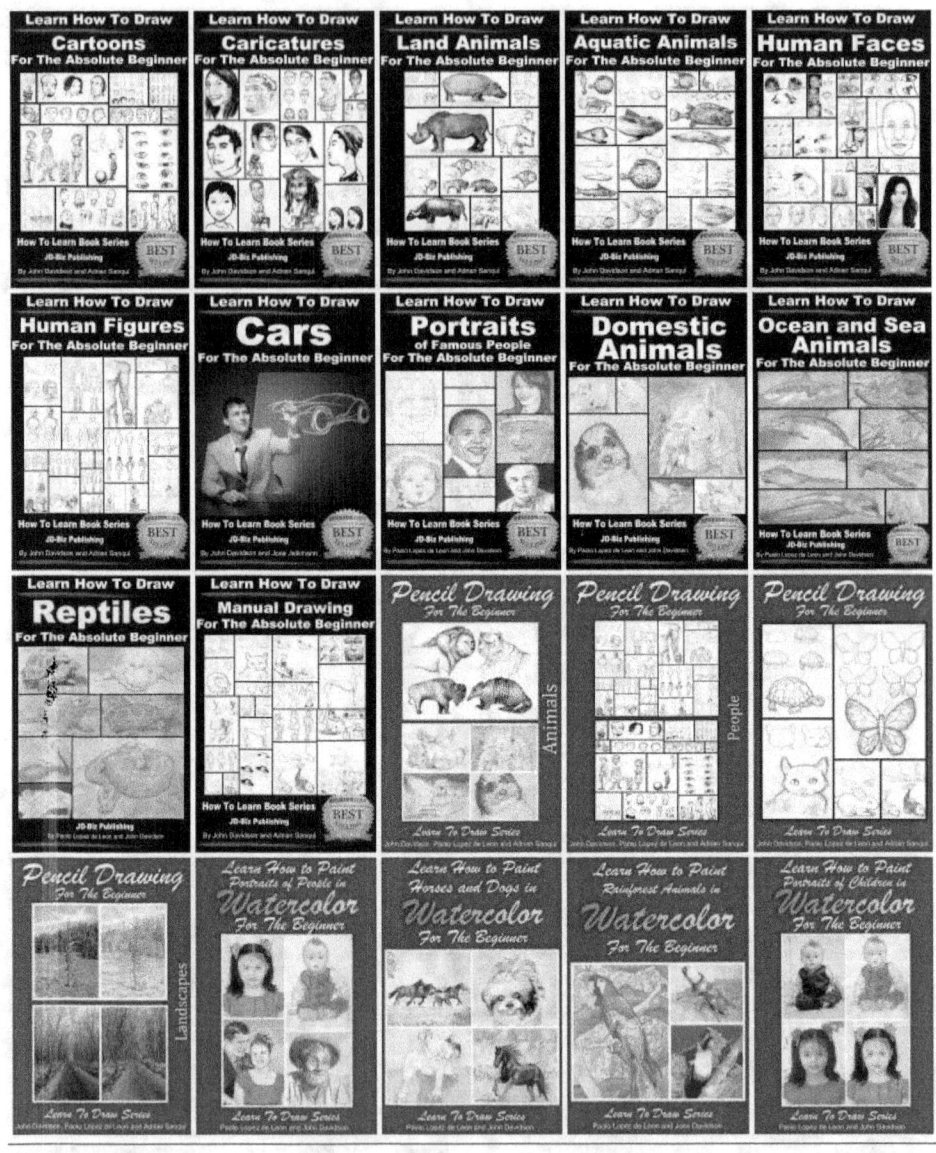

How to Build and Plan Books

Entrepreneur Book Series

Publisher

JD-Biz Corp

P O Box 374

Mendon, Utah 84325

http://www.jd-biz.com/

Mendon Cottage Books
P O Box 374, Mendon Utah 84325